I am Josephine

(and I am a living thing)

Written by
Jan Thornhill

Illustrations by
Jacqui Lee

W

FRANKLIN WATTS
LONDON • SYDNEY

I am Josephine.

I am Josephine, and
I am a human being.

I am a **human being**, and so is my mum,
and so is my dad, and so is my baby brother, Felix.

BUS
STOP

CITY BUS

How many **human beings** can you find on this page?

I am Josephine,
and I am a mammal.

I am a **mammal**, and so is my mum,
and so is my dog, Cosmo, and so is a squirrel.

And so is that cat that's always
following me around. (Shoo, kitty!)

How many different kinds of **mammals** can you find on this page?

I am Josephine,
and I am an animal.

I am an **animal**, and so is my dad,
and so is a fish, and so is a deer, and so is
that mosquito that just bit me. (Ouch!)

How many different kinds of **animals**
can you find on this page?

I am a **living thing**, and so is my brother, Felix, and so is a butterfly, and so is a tree, and so is a penguin.

How many different kinds of **living things** can you find on this page?

I am Josephine.
I am a **human being**.
I am a **mammal**.
I am an **animal**.
I am a **living thing**.

I am **all** of these things.

But I am still the only me—
Josephine!

Living things

* are made up of one or more tiny cells

* grow

* make copies of themselves (have babies)

* react to things around them

* need water and food (some make food from the Sun's energy)

* get rid of waste

* move in some way

Animals are living things that

* usually have a mother and a father (though many never know who their mothers and fathers are)

* eat other living things

* digest food in a "stomach"

* can usually move around freely

Mammals are animals that

* usually have four legs
  (or two arms and two legs
  or flippers)

* give birth to live young (except
  for a few that lay eggs)

* feed their babies milk

* have hair or fur

* have warm blood

Human beings are mammals that

* stand upright

* walk on two legs

* can do many things with their
  hands and fingers

* have large busy brains

* talk to one another about
  a million different things

* remember what happened yesterday
  and imagine what might happen
  tomorrow

* make and use complicated tools

* make art and music for the
  pure joy of it

Josephine is a **human being**...and so are **you.**
Every human being is unique, which means there is no one else on Earth who is exactly like you!

What makes **you** different from other human beings?